The Barbecue! Bible

Great Grilling Recipes from Around the World

Pearce Marion

Table Of Contents

With the multi-functionality of BBQ, you will be able to enchant your family and friends with your dishes. You will learn to enhance every flavor and be able to smoke every type of food.

Roadkill Salvage

3 tablespoons all-purpose beef
seasoning

3 tablespoons all-purpose barbeque
seasoning

2 tablespoons sumac (ground)

2 tablespoons lemon zest (grated)

3 tablespoons garlic powder

2 tablespoons granulated beef bouillon

3 tablespoons dry tomato soup mix

2 tablespoons black pepper

2 tablespoons sea salt/kosher salt

Directions:

1. In a medium bowl, mix together your
ingredients. Store in the refrigerator in
an airtight container until ready to use.

2. Rub generously onto chicken breasts,
cover and refrigerate overnight (or

minimum 4 hours) before frying,

smoking, baking, or grilling.

Chicken

3 tablespoons pumpkin pie spice

1 tablespoon lemon pepper

3 tablespoons basil

1 tablespoon dried bread crumbs

2 tablespoons granulated onion

1 tablespoon brown sugar

4 tablespoons garlic pepper

1 tablespoon marjoram

2 tablespoons black pepper

1 tablespoon sea salt/kosher salt

Directions:

1. In a medium bowl, mix together your ingredients. Store at room temperature in an airtight container until ready to use.

2. Rub generously onto chicken breasts, cover and refrigerate overnight (or

minimum 4 hours) before frying,

smoking, baking, or grilling.

Turkey Closes the

Bosphorus Strait

3 tablespoons rosemary

3 tablespoons bacon bits

1 tablespoon sumac (ground)

3 tablespoons nutmeg

1 tablespoon bay leaves (ground)

4 tablespoons dry nacho seasoning

1 tablespoon marjoram

3 tablespoons all-purpose chicken

seasoning

2 tablespoons taco seasoning mix

4 tablespoons fennel seeds

2 tablespoons sea salt/kosher salt

Directions:

1. In a medium bowl, mix together your

ingredients. Store at room temperature in

an airtight container until ready to use.

2. Rub generously onto chicken breasts, cover and refrigerate overnight (or minimum 4 hours) before frying, smoking, baking, or grilling.

Diner Dave's Chicken

Extraordinaire

1 tablespoon bacon bits

2 tablespoons taco seasoning mix

3 tablespoons sage

3 tablespoons marjoram

3 tablespoons Montreal steak spice

2 tablespoons dry nacho seasoning

1 tablespoon sumac (ground)

2 tablespoons cayenne pepper

2 tablespoons black pepper

Directions:

1. In a medium bowl, mix together your ingredients. Store at room temperature in an airtight container until ready to use.

2. Rub generously onto chicken breasts, cover and refrigerate overnight (or minimum 4 hours) before frying,

smoking, baking, or grilling.

Chicken

1 tablespoon hot curry powder

2 tablespoons dry nacho seasoning

2 tablespoons coffee beans (ground)

3 tablespoons sumac (ground)

2 tablespoons granulated garlic

1 tablespoon cinnamon

1 tablespoon dry mesquite seasoning mix

4 tablespoons thyme

1 tablespoon cardamom (ground)

2 tablespoons black pepper

1 tablespoon sea salt/kosher salt

Directions:

1. In a medium bowl, mix together your ingredients. Store at room temperature in an airtight container until ready to use.

2. Rub generously onto chicken breasts,

cover and refrigerate overnight (or

minimum 4 hours) before frying,

smoking, baking, or grilling.

Jazz is for People

3 tablespoons granulated garlic

4 tablespoons marjoram

2 tablespoons basil

1 tablespoon bay leaves (ground)

2 tablespoons cinnamon

4 tablespoons sumac (ground)

1 tablespoon mace (ground)

4 tablespoons nutmeg

2 tablespoons granulated chicken

bouillon

1 tablespoon parmesan cheese (powder

grated)

1 tablespoon black pepper

Directions:

1. In a medium bowl, mix together your

ingredients. Store in the refrigerator in

an airtight container until ready to use.

21

2. Rub generously onto chicken breasts, cover and refrigerate overnight (or minimum 4 hours) before frying, smoking, baking, or grilling.

Cruising for Alligators

1 tablespoon allspice powder

4 tablespoons granulated garlic

2 teaspoons saffron

3 tablespoons jalapeno powder

2 tablespoons cornmeal

1 tablespoon coriander seed (ground)

4 tablespoons parsley

1 tablespoon black pepper

1 tablespoon sea salt/kosher salt

Directions:

1. In a medium bowl, mix together your ingredients. Store at room temperature in an airtight container until ready to use.

2. Rub generously onto chicken breasts, cover and refrigerate overnight (or minimum 4 hours) before frying, smoking, baking, or grilling.

Dodger City

4 tablespoons all-purpose beef

seasoning

1 package instant orange drink mix

1 tablespoon nutmeg

3 tablespoons apple pie seasoning

4 tablespoons cajun seasoning

1 tablespoon hot chili powder

2 tablespoons black pepper

2 tablespoons salt

Directions:

1. In a medium bowl, mix together your

ingredients. Store at room temperature in

an airtight container until ready to use.

2. Rub generously onto chicken breasts,

cover and refrigerate overnight (or

minimum 4 hours) before frying,

smoking, baking, or grilling.

Nacho Bacon Homerun

Derby

4 tablespoons dry nacho seasoning

1 package instant orange drink mix

4 tablespoons bacon bits

1 tablespoon onion powder

4 tablespoons Chinese five-spice

powder

1 tablespoon all-purpose flour

2 tablespoons black pepper

2 tablespoons sea salt/kosher salt

Directions:

1. In a medium bowl, mix together your

ingredients. Store at room temperature in

an airtight container until ready to use.

2. Rub generously onto chicken breasts,

cover and refrigerate overnight (or

minimum 4 hours) before frying,

smoking, baking, or grilling.

Cajun Mousemeat

2 tablespoons brown sugar

3 tablespoons granulated onion

3 tablespoons savory (ground)

3 tablespoons coriander seed (ground)

6 tablespoons cajun seasoning

3 tablespoons taco seasoning mix

3 tablespoons jalapeno powder

2 tablespoons all-purpose flour

1 tablespoon sea salt/kosher salt

Directions:

1. In a medium bowl, mix together your ingredients. Store at room temperature in an airtight container until ready to use.

2. Rub generously onto chicken breasts, cover and refrigerate overnight (or minimum 4 hours) before frying, smoking, baking, or grilling.

Elite Tauren Chicken

3 tablespoons taco seasoning mix

1 tablespoon granulated onion

2 tablespoons sumac (ground)

2 tablespoons dried bread crumbs

1 tablespoon cumin

1 tablespoon cloves (ground)

2 tablespoons all-purpose chicken

seasoning

4 tablespoons parmesan cheese (powder

grated)

1 tablespoon coriander powder

1 tablespoon mace (ground)

1 tablespoon black pepper

1 tablespoon salt

Directions:

1. In a medium bowl, mix together your

ingredients. Store in the refrigerator in

an airtight container until ready to use.

2. Rub generously onto chicken breasts, cover and refrigerate overnight (or minimum 4 hours) before frying, smoking, baking, or grilling.

Killed at the Opera

4 tablespoons coriander seed (ground)

1 tablespoon Montreal steak spice

1 tablespoon mace (ground)

3 tablespoons jerk seasoning

1 tablespoon brown sugar

3 tablespoons habanero powder

2 tablespoons black pepper

1 tablespoon salt

Directions:

1. In a medium bowl, mix together your ingredients. Store at room temperature in an airtight container until ready to use.

2. Rub generously onto chicken breasts, cover and refrigerate overnight (or minimum 4 hours) before frying, smoking, baking, or grilling.

Floating in a Bathtub

3 tablespoons sage

1 tablespoon granulated onion

1 tablespoon apple pie seasoning

1 tablespoon paprika

1 tablespoon Montreal steak spice

2 tablespoons ginger (ground)

2 tablespoons black pepper

2 tablespoons sea salt/kosher salt

Directions:

1. In a medium bowl, mix together your ingredients. Store at room temperature in an airtight container until ready to use.

2. Rub generously onto chicken breasts, cover and refrigerate overnight (or minimum 4 hours) before frying, smoking, baking, or grilling.

Major Cayenne

4 tablespoons marjoram

4 tablespoons cayenne pepper

3 tablespoons bacon bits

2 teaspoons saffron

3 tablespoons lemon pepper

3 tablespoons Chinese five-spice

powder

1 tablespoon dry mesquite seasoning mix

2 tablespoons rosemary

4 tablespoons brown sugar

2 tablespoons black pepper

2 tablespoons sea salt/kosher salt

Directions:

1. In a medium bowl, mix together your

ingredients. Store at room temperature in

an airtight container until ready to use.

2. Rub generously onto chicken breasts,

cover and refrigerate overnight (or

minimum 4 hours) before frying,

smoking, baking, or grilling.

Roger's Attic Dust

1 tablespoon cilantro

4 tablespoons coriander powder

4 tablespoons garlic pepper

2 tablespoons cinnamon

1 tablespoon cloves (ground)

1 tablespoon granulated beef bouillon

Directions:

1. In a medium bowl, mix together your ingredients. Store at room temperature in an airtight container until ready to use.

2. Rub generously onto chicken breasts, cover and refrigerate overnight (or minimum 4 hours) before frying, smoking, baking, or grilling.

3 tablespoons dry french onion soup mix

1 tablespoon thyme

1 tablespoon onion powder

2 tablespoons habanero powder

2 teaspoons white pepper

2 tablespoons cornmeal

1 tablespoon black pepper

1 tablespoon salt

Directions:

1. In a medium bowl, mix together your ingredients. Store at room temperature in an airtight container until ready to use.

2. Rub generously onto chicken breasts, cover and refrigerate overnight (or minimum 4 hours) before frying, smoking, baking, or grilling.

Soccer Tournament Chicken

Surprise

1 tablespoon cilantro

1 tablespoon hot chili powder

1 tablespoon granulated chicken

bouillon

3 tablespoons Chinese five-spice

powder

4 tablespoons Montreal steak spice

2 tablespoons nutmeg

2 tablespoons ground cumin

2 tablespoons black pepper

Directions:

1. In a medium bowl, mix together your

ingredients. Store at room temperature in

an airtight container until ready to use.

2. Rub generously onto chicken breasts,

cover and refrigerate overnight (or

minimum 4 hours) before frying,

smoking, baking, or grilling.

Endangered Rhino Chicken

4 tablespoons all-purpose chicken

seasoning

2 tablespoons coriander seed (ground)

2 tablespoons burrito seasoning mix

2 tablespoons garlic powder

1 tablespoon basil

4 tablespoons Chinese five-spice

powder

3 tablespoons brown sugar

2 tablespoons coriander powder

2 tablespoons parmesan cheese (powder

grated)

2 tablespoons granulated onion

2 tablespoons black pepper

2 tablespoons sea salt/kosher salt

Directions:

1. In a medium bowl, mix together your

ingredients. Store in the refrigerator in

an airtight container until ready to use.

2. Rub generously onto chicken breasts,

cover and refrigerate overnight (or

minimum 4 hours) before frying,

smoking, baking, or grilling.

Pelican Pelican Pelican

2 tablespoons hot curry powder

4 tablespoons Montreal steak spice

1 tablespoon mace (ground)

4 tablespoons coriander powder

3 tablespoons dry french onion soup mix

1 tablespoon garlic pepper

1 tablespoon bay leaves (ground)

2 tablespoons black pepper

2 tablespoons sea salt/kosher salt

Directions:

1. In a medium bowl, mix together your ingredients. Store at room temperature in an airtight container until ready to use.

2. Rub generously onto chicken breasts, cover and refrigerate overnight (or minimum 4 hours) before frying, smoking, baking, or grilling.

Pretty Good with Lettuce

2 tablespoons parmesan cheese (powder

grated)

1 tablespoon ground cumin

1 tablespoon savory (ground)

3 tablespoons habanero powder

2 tablespoons turmeric

3 tablespoons cayenne pepper

3 tablespoons thyme

3 tablespoons lemon zest (grated)

3 tablespoons dry nacho seasoning

1 tablespoon salt

Directions:

1. In a medium bowl, mix together your

ingredients. Store in the refrigerator in

an airtight container until ready to use.

2. Rub generously onto chicken breasts,

cover and refrigerate overnight (or

minimum 4 hours) before frying,

smoking, baking, or grilling.

Band Camp Chicken

3 tablespoons dill weed

3 tablespoons cornmeal

4 tablespoons habanero powder

2 tablespoons cajun seasoning

3 tablespoons white sugar

4 tablespoons celery seed (ground)

2 teaspoons saffron

1 tablespoon cinnamon

4 tablespoons all-purpose beef

seasoning

2 tablespoons black pepper

1 tablespoon sea salt/kosher salt

Directions:

1. In a medium bowl, mix together your

ingredients. Store at room temperature in

an airtight container until ready to use.

2. Rub generously onto chicken breasts,

cover and refrigerate overnight (or

minimum 4 hours) before frying,

smoking, baking, or grilling.

Monster in the Lake

3 tablespoons cinnamon

1 tablespoon granulated chicken

bouillon

1 package instant orange drink mix

2 tablespoons hot chili powder

1 tablespoon granulated garlic

3 tablespoons hot curry powder

2 tablespoons oregano

1 tablespoon bay leaves (ground)

4 packages ranch dressing mix

2 tablespoons black pepper

Directions:

1. In a medium bowl, mix together your

ingredients. Store at room temperature in

an airtight container until ready to use.

2. Rub generously onto chicken breasts,

cover and refrigerate overnight (or

minimum 4 hours) before frying, smoking, baking, or grilling.

Chainsaw Chicken Monkey

3 tablespoons granulated beef bouillon

1 tablespoon bacon bits

2 tablespoons garlic pepper

2 tablespoons ginger (ground)

4 tablespoons all-purpose beef

seasoning

1 tablespoon cajun seasoning

4 tablespoons granulated garlic

Directions:

1. In a medium bowl, mix together your

ingredients. Store at room temperature in

an airtight container until ready to use.

2. Rub generously onto chicken breasts,

cover and refrigerate overnight (or

minimum 4 hours) before frying,

smoking, baking, or grilling.

Staircase to the Hotbox

1 tablespoon ancho chile powder

2 tablespoons garlic salt

1 tablespoon dry mustard

3 tablespoons Chinese five-spice

powder

2 tablespoons garlic powder

4 tablespoons coriander powder

1 tablespoon all-purpose seafood

seasoning

2 tablespoons fajita seasoning mix

1 tablespoon brown sugar

4 tablespoons coriander seed (ground)

2 tablespoons black pepper

Directions:

1. In a medium bowl, mix together your
ingredients. Store at room temperature in
an airtight container until ready to use.

2. Rub generously onto chicken breasts, cover and refrigerate overnight (or minimum 4 hours) before frying, smoking, baking, or grilling.

Attractive Asphalt

3 tablespoons cayenne pepper

1 tablespoon garam masala

4 tablespoons ginger (ground)

4 tablespoons coriander seed (ground)

3 tablespoons all-purpose beef

seasoning

1 tablespoon granulated onion

1 teaspoon saffron

4 tablespoons pumpkin pie spice

4 tablespoons dill weed

2 tablespoons black pepper

Directions:

1. In a medium bowl, mix together your

ingredients. Store at room temperature in

an airtight container until ready to use.

2. Rub generously onto chicken breasts,

cover and refrigerate overnight (or

minimum 4 hours) before frying,

smoking, baking, or grilling.

4 tablespoons parmesan cheese (powder grated)

1 tablespoon lemon pepper

4 tablespoons all-purpose chicken seasoning

3 tablespoons monosodium glutamate (MSG)

1 tablespoon dry mesquite seasoning mix

3 tablespoons coriander seed (ground)

1 tablespoon garlic salt

2 tablespoons black pepper

2 tablespoons sea salt/kosher salt

Directions:

1. In a medium bowl, mix together your ingredients. Store in the refrigerator in an airtight container until ready to use.

2. Rub generously onto chicken breasts,

cover and refrigerate overnight (or

minimum 4 hours) before frying,

smoking, baking, or grilling.

Don't be a Jerk to Nurses

2 tablespoons garlic pepper

1 tablespoon all-purpose barbeque seasoning

2 tablespoons all-purpose chicken seasoning

2 tablespoons dill weed

2 tablespoons cardamom (ground)

4 tablespoons jerk seasoning

2 tablespoons lemon zest (grated)

1 tablespoon Montreal steak spice

1 tablespoon garam masala

1 tablespoon black pepper

2 tablespoons sea salt/kosher salt

Directions:

1. In a medium bowl, mix together your ingredients. Store in the refrigerator in an airtight container until ready to use.

2. Rub generously onto chicken breasts, cover and refrigerate overnight (or minimum 4 hours) before frying, smoking, baking, or grilling.

3 tablespoons cayenne pepper

1 tablespoon cloves (ground)

2 tablespoons Hungarian sweet paprika

4 tablespoons jalapeno powder

3 tablespoons rosemary

2 tablespoons turmeric

3 tablespoons coffee beans (ground)

4 tablespoons sage

2 tablespoons cornmeal

3 tablespoons ginger (ground)

1 tablespoon black pepper

Directions:

1. In a medium bowl, mix together your ingredients. Store at room temperature in an airtight container until ready to use.

2. Rub generously onto chicken breasts,

cover and refrigerate overnight (or

minimum 4 hours) before frying, smoking, baking, or grilling.

Indian Tiger Mask

1 tablespoon parsley

3 tablespoons hot curry powder

2 tablespoons garam masala

2 tablespoons dry vegetarian soup mix

3 tablespoons lemon zest (grated)

4 tablespoons all-purpose chicken

seasoning

2 tablespoons monosodium glutamate

(MSG)

1 tablespoon paprika

1 tablespoon sea salt/kosher salt

Directions:

1. In a medium bowl, mix together your

ingredients. Store in the refrigerator in

an airtight container until ready to use.

2. Rub generously onto chicken breasts,

cover and refrigerate overnight (or

minimum 4 hours) before frying,

smoking, baking, or grilling.

Japanese Loan Shark

1 tablespoon hot chili powder

1 teaspoon white pepper

2 tablespoons wasabi powder

3 tablespoons parmesan cheese (powder

grated)

1 tablespoon granulated garlic

1 tablespoon Chinese five-spice powder

3 tablespoons nutmeg

4 tablespoons onion powder

1 tablespoon cornmeal

3 tablespoons coffee beans (ground)

1 tablespoon black pepper

Directions:

1. In a medium bowl, mix together your

ingredients. Store in the refrigerator in

an airtight container until ready to use.

2. Rub generously onto chicken breasts,

cover and refrigerate overnight (or minimum 4 hours) before frying, smoking, baking, or grilling.

Lady Catherine's Hat

4 tablespoons cayenne pepper

2 teaspoons saffron

2 tablespoons all-purpose barbeque

seasoning

1 tablespoon sage

1 tablespoon mace (ground)

4 tablespoons mustard seed (ground)

2 tablespoons ginger (ground)

2 tablespoons sea salt/kosher salt

Directions:

1. In a medium bowl, mix together your

ingredients. Store at room temperature in

an airtight container until ready to use.

Put on a fancy hat.

2. Rub generously onto chicken breasts,

cover and refrigerate overnight (or

minimum 4 hours) before frying,

smoking, baking, or grilling.

Yarn and Cat Chicken

2 tablespoons Montreal steak spice

1 tablespoon monosodium glutamate

(MSG)

3 tablespoons lemon pepper

4 packages ranch dressing mix

1 tablespoon rosemary

4 tablespoons sage

1 tablespoon unsweetened cocoa

powder

3 tablespoons fajita seasoning mix

2 tablespoons black pepper

2 tablespoons sea salt/kosher salt

Directions:

1. In a medium bowl, mix together your

ingredients. Store at room temperature in

an airtight container until ready to use.

2. Rub generously onto chicken breasts,

cover and refrigerate overnight (or

minimum 4 hours) before frying,

smoking, baking, or grilling.

The Rock

2 tablespoons parsley

1 tablespoon bay leaves (ground)

1 tablespoon ginger (ground)

3 tablespoons granulated garlic

2 tablespoons burrito seasoning mix

2 tablespoons coriander powder

4 tablespoons parmesan cheese (powder grated)

Directions:

1. In a medium bowl, mix together your ingredients. Store in the refrigerator in an airtight container until ready to use.

2. Rub generously onto chicken breasts, cover and refrigerate overnight (or minimum 4 hours) before frying, smoking, baking, or grilling.

Political Debate Chicken

4 tablespoons sumac (ground)

4 tablespoons garam masala

4 tablespoons oregano

1 tablespoon ginger (ground)

4 packages ranch dressing mix

2 tablespoons cardamom (ground)

3 tablespoons unsweetened cocoa

powder

1 package instant orange drink mix

1 tablespoon salt

Directions:

1. In a medium bowl, mix together your

ingredients. Store at room temperature in

an airtight container until ready to use.

2. Rub generously onto chicken breasts,

cover and refrigerate overnight (or

minimum 4 hours) before frying,

smoking, baking, or grilling.

Hangman's Rope

1 package instant orange drink mix

1 teaspoon saffron

2 tablespoons jerk seasoning

2 tablespoons bacon bits

3 tablespoons hot curry powder

1 tablespoon thyme

3 tablespoons granulated chicken

bouillon

3 tablespoons dry mustard

1 tablespoon all-purpose seafood

seasoning

1 teaspoon white pepper

1 tablespoon black pepper

1 tablespoon salt

Directions:

1. In a medium bowl, mix together your

ingredients. Store at room temperature in

an airtight container until ready to use.

2. Rub generously onto chicken breasts, cover and refrigerate overnight (or minimum 4 hours) before frying, smoking, baking, or grilling.

Over the Top

4 tablespoons turmeric

1 tablespoon coffee beans (ground)

1 tablespoon bay leaves (ground)

1 tablespoon all-purpose beef seasoning

2 tablespoons pumpkin pie spice

3 tablespoons fajita seasoning mix

2 tablespoons granulated garlic

3 tablespoons hot curry powder

4 tablespoons cardamom (ground)

2 tablespoons ancho chile powder

2 tablespoons black pepper

1 tablespoon salt

Directions:

1. In a medium bowl, mix together your ingredients. Store at room temperature in an airtight container until ready to use.

2. Rub generously onto chicken breasts,

cover and refrigerate overnight (or minimum 4 hours) before frying, smoking, baking, or grilling.

Tank Man Turbo

1 tablespoon jalapeno powder

1 package instant orange drink mix

2 tablespoons parsley

1 teaspoon saffron

1 tablespoon lemon zest (grated)

3 tablespoons cajun seasoning

4 tablespoons ginger (ground)

1 tablespoon monosodium glutamate
(MSG)

2 tablespoons celery seed (ground)

1 tablespoon sea salt/kosher salt

Directions:

1. In a medium bowl, mix together your
ingredients. Store in the refrigerator in
an airtight container until ready to use.

2. Rub generously onto chicken breasts,
cover and refrigerate overnight (or

minimum 4 hours) before frying,

smoking, baking, or grilling.

Boiling Frog Chicken

3 tablespoons pumpkin pie spice

2 tablespoons oregano

3 tablespoons fajita seasoning mix

3 tablespoons all-purpose seafood

seasoning

1 tablespoon sage

2 tablespoons hot curry powder

4 tablespoons sumac (ground)

3 tablespoons mustard seed (ground)

1 tablespoon Chinese five-spice powder

1 tablespoon coffee beans (ground)

2 tablespoons black pepper

1 tablespoon sea salt/kosher salt

Directions:

1. In a medium bowl, mix together your ingredients. Store at room temperature in an airtight container until ready to use.

2. Rub generously onto chicken breasts, cover and refrigerate overnight (or minimum 4 hours) before frying, smoking, baking, or grilling.

Lizard Tail

1 tablespoon lemon pepper

2 tablespoons celery seed (ground)

1 tablespoon hot curry powder

1 teaspoon saffron

1 tablespoon apple pie seasoning

3 tablespoons pumpkin pie spice

3 tablespoons ginger (ground)

4 tablespoons nutmeg

2 tablespoons black pepper

Directions:

1. In a medium bowl, mix together your ingredients. Store at room temperature in an airtight container until ready to use.

2. Rub generously onto chicken breasts, cover and refrigerate overnight (or minimum 4 hours) before frying, smoking, baking, or grilling.

Grasshopper Fajita

3 tablespoons fajita seasoning mix

3 tablespoons cumin

3 tablespoons coriander

2 tablespoons sumac (ground)

2 tablespoons dry vegetarian soup mix

1 tablespoon dry mesquite seasoning mix

3 tablespoons cajun seasoning

4 tablespoons garlic powder

3 tablespoons fennel seeds

1 tablespoon black pepper

2 tablespoons salt

Directions:

1. In a medium bowl, mix together your ingredients. Store at room temperature in an airtight container until ready to use.

2. Rub generously onto chicken breasts, cover and refrigerate overnight (or

minimum 4 hours) before frying,

smoking, baking, or grilling.

English Invasion Chicken

2 teaspoons saffron

2 tablespoons savory (ground)

2 tablespoons Montreal steak spice

2 tablespoons rosemary

2 tablespoons nutmeg

3 tablespoons allspice powder

2 tablespoons burrito seasoning mix

1 tablespoon marjoram

4 tablespoons fennel seeds

2 tablespoons all-purpose chicken

seasoning

2 tablespoons black pepper

1 tablespoon salt

Directions:

1. In a medium bowl, mix together your

ingredients. Store at room temperature in

an airtight container until ready to use.

2. Rub generously onto chicken breasts, cover and refrigerate overnight (or minimum 4 hours) before frying, smoking, baking, or grilling.

Barking Dog

1 tablespoon turmeric

2 tablespoons cajun seasoning

2 tablespoons all-purpose barbeque

seasoning

1 tablespoon all-purpose chicken

seasoning

4 tablespoons cardamom (ground)

4 tablespoons bacon bits

4 tablespoons apple pie seasoning

3 tablespoons mustard seed (ground)

2 tablespoons sea salt/kosher salt

Directions:

1. In a medium bowl, mix together your

ingredients. Store at room temperature in

an airtight container until ready to use.

2. Rub generously onto chicken breasts,

cover and refrigerate overnight (or

minimum 4 hours) before frying,

smoking, baking, or grilling.

Annoying Squirrel

3 tablespoons coriander powder

3 tablespoons black peppercorns

(coarsely ground)

4 tablespoons coffee beans (ground)

1 tablespoon cloves (ground)

3 tablespoons taco seasoning mix

3 tablespoons fennel seeds

1 tablespoon all-purpose beef seasoning

1 tablespoon dill weed

2 tablespoons dry nacho seasoning

1 tablespoon Chinese five-spice powder

2 tablespoons black pepper

2 tablespoons salt

Directions:

1. In a medium bowl, mix together your ingredients. Store at room temperature in an airtight container until ready to use.

2. Rub generously onto chicken breasts, cover and refrigerate overnight (or minimum 4 hours) before frying, smoking, baking, or grilling.

Miniskirt Lesbian Spice

1 package instant orange drink mix

2 tablespoons mustard seed (ground)

2 tablespoons all-purpose flour

3 tablespoons cilantro

1 tablespoon dry mesquite seasoning mix

1 tablespoon paprika

4 tablespoons cornmeal

3 tablespoons parsley

4 tablespoons thyme

3 tablespoons brown sugar

2 tablespoons black pepper

2 tablespoons sea salt/kosher salt

Directions:

1. In a medium bowl, mix together your ingredients. Store at room temperature in an airtight container until ready to use.

2. Rub generously onto chicken breasts,

cover and refrigerate overnight (or
minimum 4 hours) before frying,
smoking, baking, or grilling.

Time for a Nuclear Blast

4 tablespoons jalapeno powder

4 tablespoons hot curry powder

2 tablespoons cayenne pepper

4 tablespoons unsweetened cocoa
powder

3 tablespoons sumac (ground)

3 tablespoons Hungarian sweet paprika

1 tablespoon onion powder

1 tablespoon mace (ground)

1 tablespoon bacon bits

3 tablespoons dry mustard

3 tablespoons dried bread crumbs

1 tablespoon dry nacho seasoning

2 tablespoons black pepper

1 tablespoon sea salt/kosher salt

Directions:

1. In a medium bowl, mix together your
ingredients. Store at room temperature in
an airtight container until ready to use.

2. Rub generously onto chicken breasts,
cover and refrigerate overnight (or
minimum 4 hours) before frying,
smoking, baking, or grilling.

Ghostbuster Chicken

2 tablespoons garlic powder

4 tablespoons cajun seasoning

2 tablespoons dry mustard

2 tablespoons brown sugar

1 tablespoon cilantro

1 tablespoon cloves (ground)

3 tablespoons granulated chicken

bouillon

1 tablespoon nutmeg

1 package instant orange drink mix

2 tablespoons black pepper

1 tablespoon sea salt/kosher salt

Directions:

1. In a medium bowl, mix together your

ingredients. Store at room temperature in

an airtight container until ready to use.

2. Rub generously onto chicken breasts,

cover and refrigerate overnight (or

minimum 4 hours) before frying,

smoking, baking, or grilling.

Lazy Jedi

2 tablespoons hot chili powder

1 tablespoon pumpkin pie spice

2 tablespoons Chinese five-spice
powder

1 tablespoon sumac (ground)

2 tablespoons habanero powder

2 tablespoons red pepper flakes

4 tablespoons granulated beef bouillon

2 tablespoons turmeric

3 tablespoons granulated garlic

1 tablespoon taco seasoning mix

2 tablespoons black pepper

Directions:

1. In a medium bowl, mix together your

ingredients. Store at room temperature in

an airtight container until ready to use.

2. Rub generously onto chicken breasts,

cover and refrigerate overnight (or

minimum 4 hours) before frying,

smoking, baking, or grilling.

Ugly Llama Nacho Chicken

2 tablespoons lemon zest (grated)

4 tablespoons coffee beans (ground)

1 tablespoon granulated garlic

2 tablespoons all-purpose barbeque

seasoning

5 tablespoons dry nacho seasoning

1 tablespoon cilantro

1 tablespoon sea salt/kosher salt

Directions:

1. In a medium bowl, mix together your

ingredients. Store in the refrigerator in

an airtight container until ready to use.

2. Rub generously onto chicken breasts,

cover and refrigerate overnight (or

minimum 4 hours) before frying,

smoking, baking, or grilling.

Chinese Fence Attack

4 tablespoons sage

4 tablespoons Chinese five-spice

powder

1 tablespoon savory (ground)

1 tablespoon sumac (ground)

2 tablespoons jalapeno powder

3 tablespoons taco seasoning mix

1 tablespoon black pepper

2 tablespoons sea salt/kosher salt

Directions:

1. In a medium bowl, mix together your

ingredients. Store at room temperature in

an airtight container until ready to use.

2. Rub generously onto chicken breasts,

cover and refrigerate overnight (or

minimum 4 hours) before frying,

smoking, baking, or grilling.

Total Security

2 tablespoons granulated garlic

2 tablespoons ground cumin

2 tablespoons garlic pepper

2 tablespoons paprika

4 tablespoons dill weed

2 tablespoons coffee beans (ground)

1 tablespoon Chinese five-spice powder

2 tablespoons all-purpose chicken
seasoning

4 tablespoons unsweetened cocoa
powder

3 tablespoons parmesan cheese (powder
grated)

2 tablespoons black pepper

1 tablespoon sea salt/kosher salt

Directions:

1. In a medium bowl, mix together your

ingredients. Store in the refrigerator in

an airtight container until ready to use.

2. Rub generously onto chicken breasts,

cover and refrigerate overnight (or

minimum 4 hours) before frying,

smoking, baking, or grilling.

CPSIA information can be obtained
at www.ICGtesting.com
Printed in the USA
BVHW090031240521
607981BV00002B/149

9 781802 834932